The Usborne book of
PLANET EARTH

Written by
Megan Cullis & Matthew Oldham

Illustrated by
Stephanie Fizer Coleman

Designed by
Emily Barden

USBORNE QUICKLINKS

For links to websites where you can explore
Planet Earth with virtual tours, video clips and
activities, go to the Usborne Quicklinks website
at **www.usborne.com/quicklinks** and type in the
title of this book. Please follow the online safety
guidelines at the Usborne Quicklinks website.
We recommend children are supervised online.

THE ADVENTURE BEGINS

This book will take you on a spectacular journey all around our home, Planet Earth. Follow the red string on this map of the world to see where you'll be stopping on your amazing adventure.

EUROPE

Fiery volcano

NORTH AMERICA

City at night

Flooded wetland

Towering forests

Stormy plains

Dusty desert

YOUR JOURNEY STARTS HERE

Steamy jungle

Isolated islands

ATLANTIC OCEAN

Lake in the mountains

These pins mark each stop on your journey.

The land on Planet Earth is divided into seven huge areas known as continents. Each chapter in this book visits a new continent.

SOUTH AMERICA

PACIFIC OCEAN

Planet Earth has five vast bodies of water called oceans. They all join up together.

SOUTHERN OCEAN

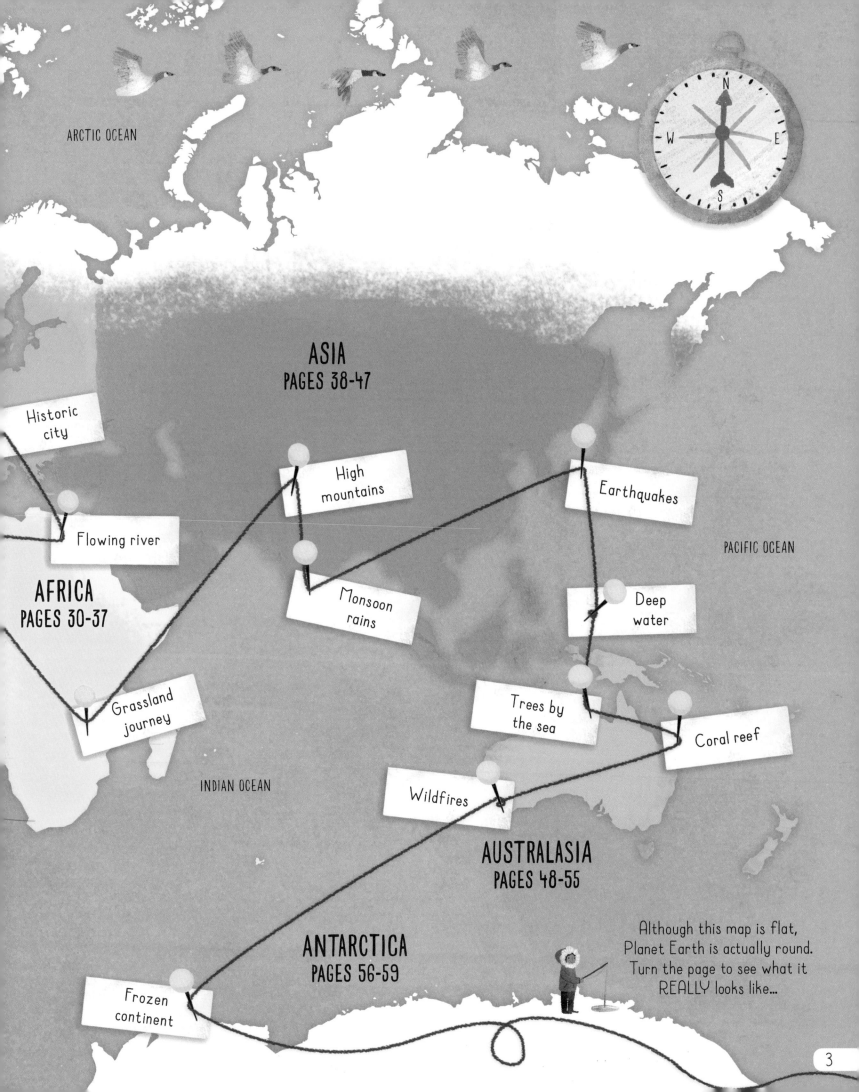

ARCTIC OCEAN

ASIA
PAGES 38-47

Historic city

Flowing river

High mountains

Earthquakes

PACIFIC OCEAN

AFRICA
PAGES 30-37

Monsoon rains

Deep water

Grassland journey

Trees by the sea

Coral reef

INDIAN OCEAN

Wildfires

AUSTRALASIA
PAGES 48-55

Although this map is flat, Planet Earth is actually round. Turn the page to see what it REALLY looks like...

ANTARCTICA
PAGES 56-59

Frozen continent

THIS IS PLANET EARTH

We live on a planet called Earth, a huge, spinning ball of rock that moves around and around a fiery star called the Sun. Our world is one of eight planets locked in this dizzying dance. Together, they make up the Solar System.

These lines show the route Earth and its nearest planets take as they move around the Sun.

EARTH

This is how Earth might look if you went up in a spaceship.

MOON

On Earth we have just the right amount of warmth and light from the Sun, air to breathe, and water for living things to grow.

SUN

This is the Sun. It's an enormous ball of hot gases that give out light and heat to all the planets in the Solar System.

MERCURY

VENUS

Mercury and Venus are much closer to the Sun than Earth. It's probably too hot for living things to survive on these planets.

There are trillions and trillions of planets beyond our Solar System, but Earth is the only one that we know of to have living things on it.

Earth has a smaller ball of rock that moves around it – this is the Moon.

It's probably too cold for living things to survive on Mars. It's much colder than our planet because it's further away from the Sun.

MARS

Turn the page to come back down to Planet Earth and take the first steps of your epic journey around the world...

KEY

There is a map of each continent in this book. Here are some of the things to look out for on them.

 Mountains and other very high places

 Rivers, lakes and other areas of water

 Deserts and very dry places

 Grassy areas or grasslands

 Forests and jungles in warm, wet places

 Forests in places with cool winters

 Forests where it's cold all year

 Places covered by snow and ice

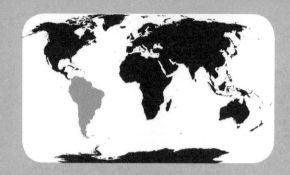

Brown pelican

SOUTH AMERICA

THE ENCHANTED ISLANDS, pages 8-9
Many of the plants and animals that live on the isolated Galápagos Islands aren't found anywhere else in the world.

LAKE AT THE TOP OF THE WORLD, pages 10-11
People have been living on Lake Titicaca, high up in the mountains, since ancient times.

The soil in the Atacama Desert is similar to samples taken from Mars, so scientists use the desert to test vehicles and tools to be used in space.

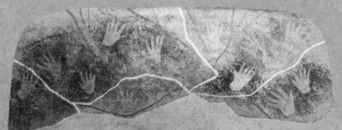

Ancient hand prints cover the stone walls of the Cave of the Hands in Argentina. People painted them more than 9,500 years ago.

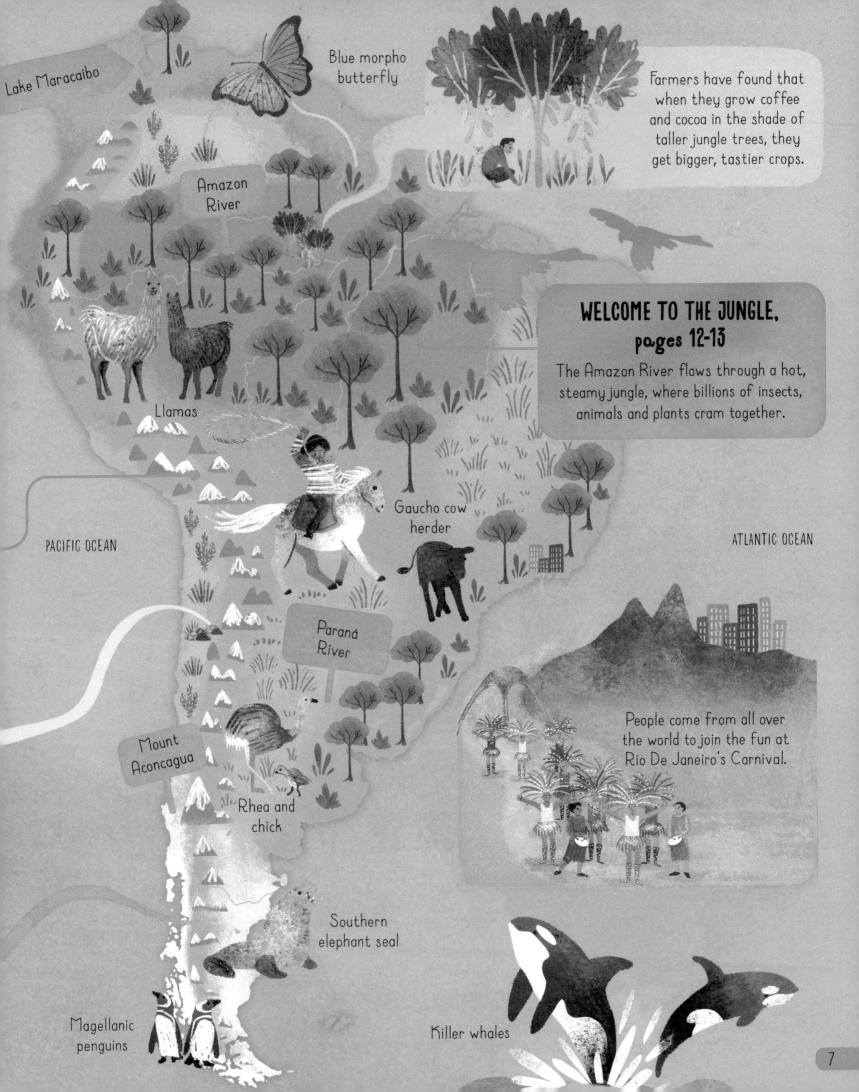

Lake Maracaibo

Blue morpho butterfly

Farmers have found that when they grow coffee and cocoa in the shade of taller jungle trees, they get bigger, tastier crops.

Amazon River

WELCOME TO THE JUNGLE,
pages 12-13
The Amazon River flows through a hot, steamy jungle, where billions of insects, animals and plants cram together.

Llamas

PACIFIC OCEAN

ATLANTIC OCEAN

Gaucho cow herder

Paraná River

People come from all over the world to join the fun at Rio De Janeiro's Carnival.

Mount Aconcagua

Rhea and chick

Southern elephant seal

Magellanic penguins

Killer whales

THE ENCHANTED ISLANDS

Hundreds of miles off the coast of South America, in the Pacific Ocean, there lies a remote cluster of wild, rocky islands - the Galápagos Islands. Many animals and plants that live there are found nowhere else on Planet Earth.

Marine iguanas nibble on seaweed under the water. They are the only lizards in the world that live on land but find their food in the sea.

The islands' sandy beaches are perfect sunbathing spots for the world's smallest type of sea lion – the Galápagos sea lion.

Galápagos penguins speed through the cool waters, catching small fish. No other penguins are found in the wild this far north on Planet Earth.

8

Spanish explorers named the islands "the Enchanted Isles" when they first discovered them in the 16th century. No people lived there – just animals.

FAMOUS FINDINGS

In 1835, an English scientist named Charles Darwin visited the Galápagos Islands to study the local wildlife. Several years later, he published a book about his findings which made him famous.

Darwin studied the differences between 15 types of finches that live on the islands.

Green warbler-finch

Large ground finch

Vampire ground finch

These islands are separated from any other land by nearly 1,000km (620 miles) of ocean.

Flightless cormorants swim around the islands using their short, stubby wings. There are lots of types of cormorants in the world – but these are the only ones that can't fly.

Huge, spiky plants called Galápagos prickly pears are scattered across the islands. They can grow taller than a person.

Among the tall grasses, Galápagos tortoises plod along, grazing on leaves. They are the world's biggest tortoises, and can live for over 100 years.

LAKE AT THE TOP OF THE WORLD

Nestled among snowy mountain peaks in the Andes, Lake Titicaca is one of the highest lakes on Earth. Its sparkling blue waters are scattered with islands of all sizes, where people have lived since ancient times.

UROS FLOATING ISLANDS

The Uros people live on a group of floating islands they've made out of reeds.

Each floating island is secured to the bottom of the lake with ropes.

ANY LUCK FISHING TODAY?

YES, THANKS, I HAD A GREAT CATCH!

Every month, people lay a fresh layer of reeds on top of the old ones.

Titicaca grebe

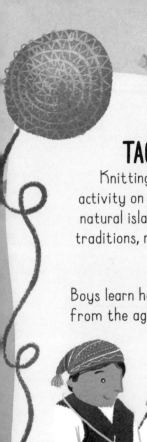

TAQUILE ISLAND

Knitting and weaving is a daily activity on Taquile – one of the lake's natural islands. According to Taquile's traditions, men knit and women weave.

Wool cloth is woven on wooden looms.

Boys learn how to knit from the age of eight.

WILL I EVER BE AS GOOD AS YOU?

THE TRICK IS TO BE PATIENT.

This man is knitting a hat called a chullo.

His woven waistband is decorated with flowers and birds.

ISLA DEL SOL

This is another natural island on Lake Titicaca. Potatoes, which originated on the slopes of the Andes, are grown all over the island.

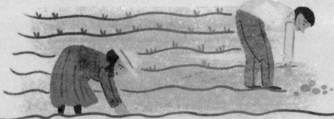

Potato plant

Islanders hold a potato festival every year. They believe the celebrations will bring a good harvest.

I'M WORN OUT.

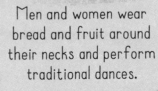

Men and women wear bread and fruit around their necks and perform traditional dances.

WELCOME TO THE JUNGLE

Billions of creatures crowd together in a dark, noisy jungle that stretches for miles on either side of the Amazon River. This is the biggest jungle on Planet Earth.

Brazil nut tree

Mahogany tree

Orchids

Rubber tree

Jungles are thick forests that grow in warm, wet places. They're also known as tropical rainforests.

Many of our medicines come from Amazon plants. For instance, bark from Pink Trumpet trees can be used to treat cancer.

Plants beneath the trees have big, flat leaves to soak up any sunlight that shines through.

LEAFY LAYERS

Different animals live in different layers of the forest.

Macaws

Harpy eagle

Most of the animals that live in the highest branches hardly ever touch the ground.

Capuchin monkeys

Emerald tree boa

Red-eyed tree frog

Howler monkeys

OOOH OOH...

The tree tops form a canopy that covers the forest below. Many animals live in this layer, where there are lots of fruits and nuts to eat.

Brazilian porcupine

Sloth

Sword-billed hummingbird

Animals that live in the dappled shade beneath the canopy often have markings that help them blend with their surroundings.

Green malachite butterflies

Cocoa tree

Iguana

Jaguar

On the forest floor, insects and animals live among a tangle of roots and dead leaves.

Giant anteater

Leafcutter ants

Armadillo

Skeleton tarantula

LEFT, RIGHT, LEFT RIGHT...

Blue fungi

13

Caribou

Denali (formerly Mount McKinley)

The mighty peaks of the Rocky Mountains sit side by side in a row that stretches for thousands of miles.

Bear

Missouri River

IN THE LAND OF GIANTS, pages 16-17
The tallest trees in the world grow in the redwood forests of California.

Bald eagle

BIG SKY COUNTRY, pages 18-19
Huge, sweeping grasslands lie under stormy skies in the Great Plains.

PACIFIC OCEAN

The Colorado River carves its way between the steep, plunging sides of the Grand Canyon.

Loggerhead sea turtle

Canada geese

Harp seals

Hudson Bay

NORTH AMERICA

The Great Lakes

Mississippi River

Buffalo

Toucan

Gulf of Mexico

ATLANTIC OCEAN

BRIGHT LIGHTS, BIG CITY, pages 20-21
New York City is known as "the city that never sleeps" because it's almost as busy at night as it is during the day.

Alligators lurk among cypress trees and tall grasses in flat, swampy wetlands called the Everglades.

Caribbean Sea

Thick, lush jungle grows around the ruins of Chichén Itzá, an ancient city that's over 1,500 years old.

IN THE LAND OF GIANTS

The coasts of Northern California are foggy and mild all year. It's in this gentle, damp setting that monumental forests, unlike any others found on Earth, have been able to grow.

These are coastal redwoods, the tallest trees on the planet.

Coastal redwoods can grow taller than a 30-floor skyscraper.

Redwoods are evergreens, so their branches stay covered in delicate green needles all year round.

These tall trunks protect branches and needles from fires on the forest floor.

CAW CAW

Bald eagle

The fog keeps these trees cool and moist all year round – without it they couldn't survive.

Redwood forests are often cloaked in sea fog that rolls in from the Pacific Ocean.

This is a flying squirrel. These animals don't really fly, but they use flaps of skin on either side of their bodies to glide around.

WOOSH

Redwoods are among the oldest living things on Earth...

...they can live to be over 2,000 years old.

Forest creatures of all sizes live in hollows left behind by forest fires.

REDWOOD ANIMALS THROUGH THE YEAR

Near the end of summer, male elks fight each other to get the attention of female elks.

During the winter, a bobcat's fur starts to fade. This helps it blend in with bare branches on the forest floor.

In the spring, bear cubs leave their dens and take their first steps in the forest.

BIG SKY COUNTRY

The middle of North America is covered by a huge area of sweeping grassland called the Great Plains. This is a windswept land of endless horizons, where the weather can be dramatic, destructive and sometimes explosive...

When the sun shines down on the Great Plains, the ground heats up, and warm air rises into the sky.

Tall thunderclouds like this often make sparks of electricity called lightning. These sparks can flash in the sky or strike the ground.

This warm air climbs higher and higher, until it meets cold, dry air that blows over the Rocky Mountains.

These are the perfect conditions for violent, spinning winds called tornadoes, or twisters.

The Rocky Mountains

TWISTER! CLOSE THE SHELTER DOORS.

Some people call this part of America Tornado Alley.

Tornado shelter

When cold air and warm air meet, they make tall clouds that pile high into the sky.

Inside the cloud, the warm air and the cold air start to spin around each other...

...they spin faster and faster and the cloud changes shape...

...to become a tornado that hits the ground.

Tornadoes can rip up crops and even destroy buildings as they sweep across the land.

DOG TOWN

Many animals on the Great Plains live in underground burrows where they can shelter from the extreme weather.

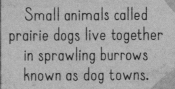

Small animals called prairie dogs live together in sprawling burrows known as dog towns.

Prairie dogs aren't really dogs – they're actually a type of squirrel.

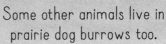

Some other animals live in prairie dog burrows too.

Prairie rattlesnake

Burrowing owl

BRIGHT LIGHTS, BIG CITY

Honk, honk! Beeeep! New York City is busy day and night. It's home to an incredible 8 million people – and some of the world's tallest buildings, known as skyscrapers.

HELLO THERE AND WELCOME TO NEW YORK!

One World Trade Center

New York is surrounded by water. Most of the city is built on three islands – Long Island, Staten Island and Manhattan.

A giant copper statue watches over the city from afar. It's called the Statue of Liberty.

Towering skyscrapers cram together on the island of Manhattan.

Flatiron Building

LAND AHOY!

HEY! CAREFUL, BUDDY.

VROOM

Brooklyn Bridge is the oldest of the bridges that stretch across the East River.

Williamsburg Bridge

Manhattan Bridge

Brooklyn Heights Promenade

Peregrine falcons swoop and dive between skyscrapers, chasing pigeons below.

NEW JERSEY

CAW CAW

Empire State Building

Chrysler Building

There's not much space on the ground – so buildings have grown tall instead of wide.

HUDSON RIVER

American Museum of Natural History

MMM, BAGEL.

In Central Park, New Yorkers can take a walk, skate around on ice rinks and even visit animals at a zoo.

WHEE!

Times Square

THE TRAFFIC'S TERRIBLE TONIGHT.

SUBWAY

Metropolitan Museum of Art

The Guggenheim

Yellow taxicabs roar through the city streets.

EAST RIVER

ROOSEVELT ISLAND

Queensboro Bridge

SUBWAY

New Yorkers hurry around the city on the New York Subway – a giant network of underground trains.

NEXT STOP: HIGH STREET, BROOKLYN BRIDGE!

EUROPE

Norwegian Sea

BLOWING UP! pages 24-25
Iceland has over 100 volcanoes – they can be fiery and explosive, but they also bring many advantages to the people who live there.

Reindeer stag

North Sea

ATLANTIC OCEAN

Rivers tumble from the top of limestone cliffs down into the turquoise waters of the Plitvice Lakes in Croatia.

Sheep

AFTER THE FLOOD, pages 26-27
The Doñana National Park is an enormous wetland in the south of Spain, where millions of water birds come to find food and shelter.

Mont Blanc

Bay of Biscay

Asturian cattle

Pyrenean goat

CITY OF WATER, pages 28-30
Palaces and churches line busy canals in Venice, a historic city that seems to float on water.

Husky sleigh

Volga River

All along this coast, thin fingers of steep, rocky land reach out into the North Sea, creating spectacular valleys called fjords.

Wolves roam free in Białowieża Forest, an ancient wilderness that stretches across parts of Poland and Belarus.

Mount Elbrus

River Danube

In the Koyashskoye Salt Lake, just off the north coast of the Black Sea, tiny plants have turned the water bright pink.

Black Sea

Ancient monuments and temples perch on rocky cliffs that tower over the modern city streets of Athens.

Mediterranean Sea

BLOWING UP!

Every fifty years or so, something stirs deep below the Icelandic mountain of Bárðarbunga. First, the snowy peak begins to sizzle and hiss. Then, KABOOM! Red-hot rocks fly like canonballs and clouds of smoke pile into the sky. Bárðarbunga isn't just a mountain... it's also a volcano.

Volcanoes are openings in the Earth's surface, where hot, sticky rock from deep underneath bursts through...

When this happens it's called a volcanic eruption.

The red-hot rock that comes out is called lava.

Volcanic eruptions often cause big explosions that look like this.

It's not just lava that escapes – poisonous gases, clouds of ash and chunks of solid rock are also forced out.

Like many other volcanoes, Bárðarbunga has steep slopes made from layers of hardened lava and ash. Each time it erupts, more layers pile up, and the mountain grows a bit taller.

Bárðarbunga isn't the only volcano in Iceland. There are more than 100 others, although some don't erupt any more.

DEEP SECRETS

Volcanoes offer scientists a glimpse of what happens deep under the ground.

The surface of Planet Earth is covered by a thin layer of rock known as the crust. It runs underneath the oceans and rises up to make land.

Iceland

Iceland sits above large cracks in the Earth's crust that fill up with hot rock from underneath.

Ocean

Crust

Below the crust is a much thicker layer of hot, squishy rock known as the mantle.

The mantle is very, very hot – the hottest, deepest parts are 4,000°C (7,230°F).

IN THE VOLCANO'S SHADOW

Volcanic eruptions are very dangerous – but they also bring many advantages to people who live nearby.

Iceland's power stations use heat from the mantle to make electricity and warm up people's homes.

This is called geothermal energy.

MMM. STEAMY.

AHHH!

People from all over the world come to Iceland to visit its hot springs, where water under the ground has been warmed by the mantle.

Ash from past eruptions makes the soil especially rich for growing crops.

AFTER THE FLOOD

Wetlands, such as the Doñana National Park in Spain, are areas where the ground is often flooded or full of water. They're interesting, changeable places where muddy islands disappear and reappear as flood waters rise and fall.

Rivers from far away feed into the Doñana, bringing water and mud into the park.

Winter rains make the rivers overflow and the whole area floods.

Wetland plants have long stems that poke above the water so they can survive the flooded conditions.

In the spring, the winter floods start to fall back, revealing vast expanses of mud.

This mud is full of shellfish, worms and insects – the perfect food for flamingos and other wetland birds.

BIRDS OF THE DOÑANA

Egret

Purple heron

Ibis

Spoonbill

Squacco heron

Black-winged stilt

Many Doñana birds have long legs to wade through the water, and long beaks to poke around in the mud.

Flamingos

Every spring, over 10,000 flamingos fly into the park after spending the winter in warmer countries further south.

Marsh horses

Rice field

Birds all over the world rely on wetlands where they find food, shelter and safe places to have babies.

Millions of birds descend upon this park every year.

Other birds have shorter beaks to help them catch flying insects.

Wetland birds often spend as much time swimming as they do wading and flying.

Sandgrouse

Bee-eater

Marbled teal

Collared pratincole

Hoopoe

Crested coot

Whiskered terns build nests that float on the water.

27

CITY OF WATER

Welcome to Venice, a city built on muddy islands
in the middle of a huge, sheltered lagoon in Northern Italy.
People from all over the world come to stroll along
its historic canals, lined with tall towers
and grand, marble palaces.

Santi Apostoli

Only 55,000 people live
in Venice permanently, but
more than 20 million tourists
visit every year.

This is the
Rialto Bridge – it
crosses the Grand Canal,
the city's main canal.

ALL ABOARD!

Police boat

Traditional Venetian
boat, known as a gondola

HELLO VENICE!

Known as "The Floating City" to some,
Venice doesn't actually float. All of its
buildings sit on top of long wooden stilts so
they don't sink into the soft mud below.

Vaporetti, or
water bus

There are seven main areas of Venice, spread over 118 tiny islands, linked by a maze of canals.

- Dorsodouro
- Cannaregio
- Santa Croce
- San Polo
- San Marco
- Castello
- Giudecca

San Bartolomeo di Rialto

The city of Venice is sinking, very slowly, into the mud. It sinks by about 4cm (1.6 inches) every 10 years.

There are no cars in Venice – people travel around on boats instead.

Postal delivery boat

A world-famous carnival is held every year. People parade the streets wearing elaborate masks and costumes.

IT'S HOT UNDER HERE!

AFRICA

Hooded vulture

Atlas Mountains

Spiny-tailed lizard

Sitting in the foothills of the Atlas Mountains, Aït-Ben-Haddou is an ancient walled village built from mud bricks.

HOT DAYS...COOL NIGHTS, pages 34-35

Snakes slither and insects scuttle across the sand in the dusty Sahara Desert.

A type of whale called Bryde's whale

ATLANTIC OCEAN

An enormous, flat-topped mountain, called Table Mountain, overlooks the city of Cape Town.

The sea around the southern coast of Africa is very stormy, and the waters are difficult for ships to sail.

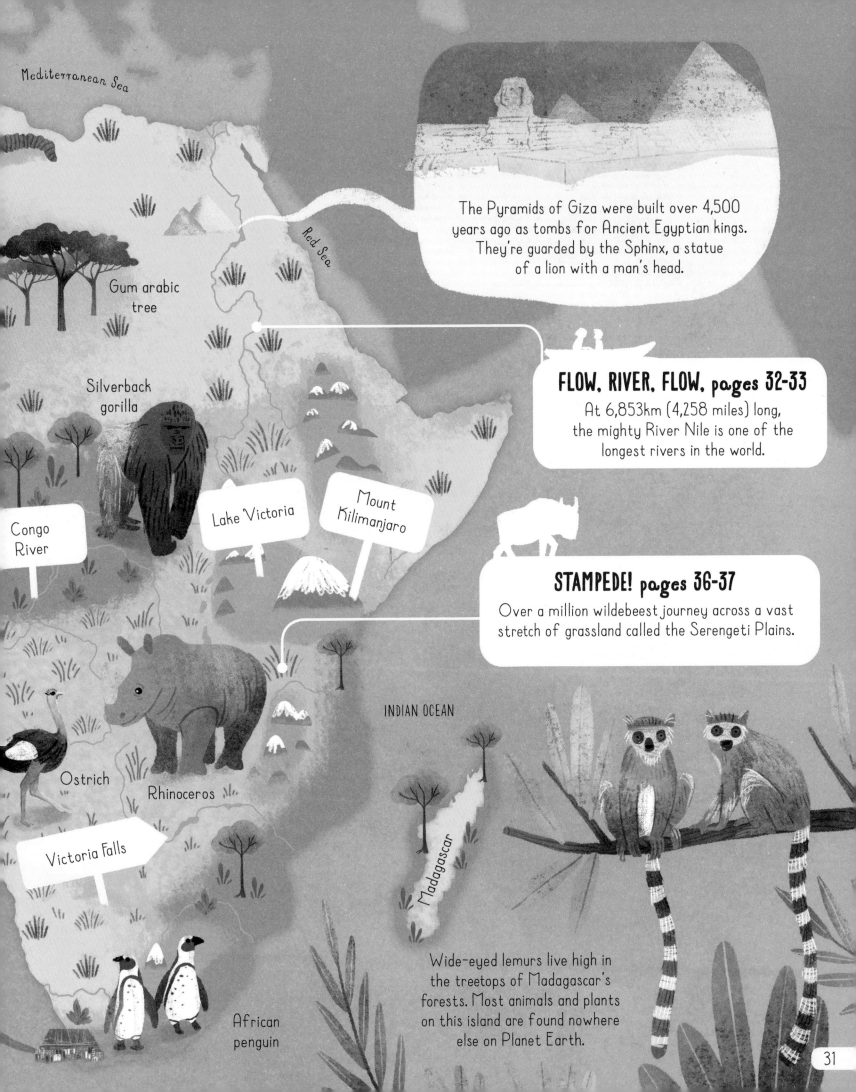

Mediterranean Sea

Red Sea

The Pyramids of Giza were built over 4,500 years ago as tombs for Ancient Egyptian kings. They're guarded by the Sphinx, a statue of a lion with a man's head.

Gum arabic tree

Silverback gorilla

FLOW, RIVER, FLOW, pages 32-33
At 6,853km (4,258 miles) long, the mighty River Nile is one of the longest rivers in the world.

Congo River

Lake Victoria

Mount Kilimanjaro

STAMPEDE! pages 36-37
Over a million wildebeest journey across a vast stretch of grassland called the Serengeti Plains.

INDIAN OCEAN

Ostrich

Rhinoceros

Madagascar

Victoria Falls

Wide-eyed lemurs live high in the treetops of Madagascar's forests. Most animals and plants on this island are found nowhere else on Planet Earth.

African penguin

FLOW, RIVER, FLOW

The River Nile is one of the longest rivers in the world. Winding down mountains and gushing across deserts, it flows through eleven countries until it reaches the Mediterranean Sea.

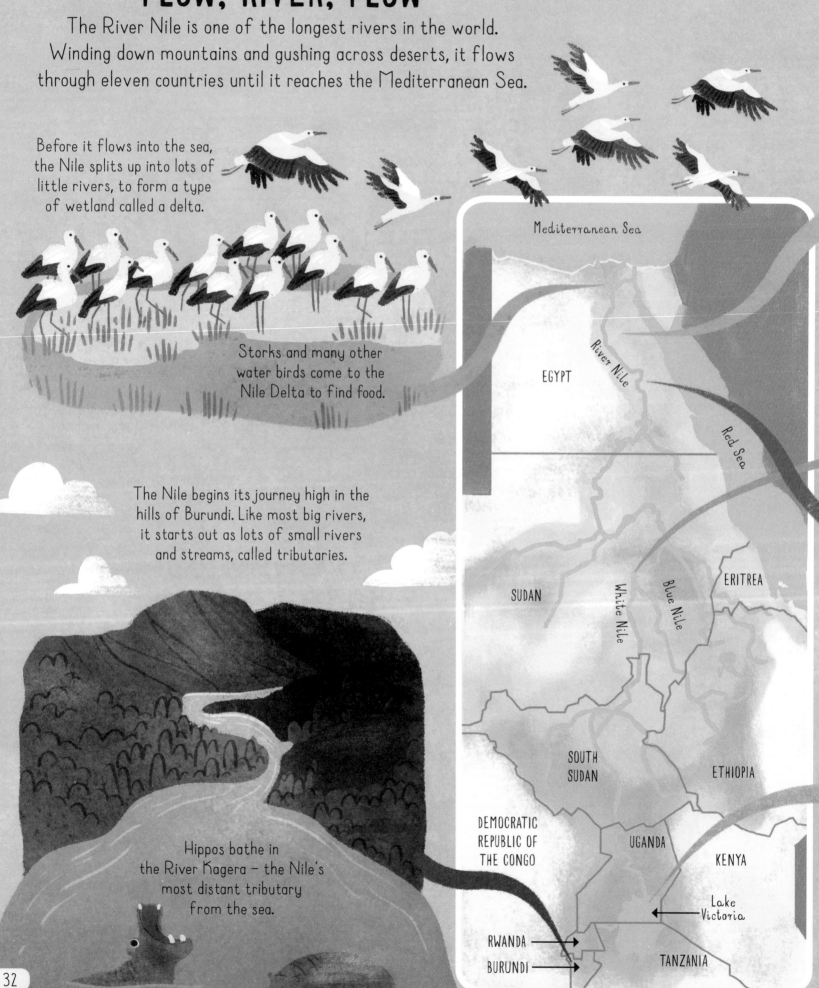

Before it flows into the sea, the Nile splits up into lots of little rivers, to form a type of wetland called a delta.

Storks and many other water birds come to the Nile Delta to find food.

The Nile begins its journey high in the hills of Burundi. Like most big rivers, it starts out as lots of small rivers and streams, called tributaries.

Hippos bathe in the River Kagera – the Nile's most distant tributary from the sea.

Mediterranean Sea

EGYPT

River Nile

Red Sea

SUDAN

White Nile

Blue Nile

ERITREA

SOUTH SUDAN

ETHIOPIA

DEMOCRATIC REPUBLIC OF THE CONGO

UGANDA

KENYA

Lake Victoria

RWANDA

BURUNDI

TANZANIA

The Nile snakes through Egypt, cutting across barren deserts. But its muddy banks are very fertile, and well suited for growing crops.

Sugar cane grows here. It's used to make sugar.

Two big tributaries meet in Sudan. The Blue Nile is very muddy so it almost looks black. The White Nile is full of ground-up rock, so it almost looks white. When they mix together, the river grows wider.

Huge sandstone buildings stand along the banks of the Nile. Many were built around 3,500 years ago.

In Uganda, thousands of little streams and rivers tumble down into Lake Victoria, Africa's largest lake.

Around 35 million people rely on Lake Victoria as a source of drinking water and food.

Nile crocodiles prowl along the shores of the lake.

HOT DAYS...

Great clouds of dust and sand blow across the Sahara, the biggest – and hottest – desert on Planet Earth. This is a land of extremes, where scorching hot days turn into freezing cold nights in a matter of hours...

A desert is a dry area of land where there's hardly any rainfall.

Sand blows across the ground, piling up into big hills, called dunes.

Many people who live in the Sahara don't have fixed homes – they travel around in groups, looking for food and water.

KEEP GOING, EVERYONE!

Strong winds whip up the sand into hot, swirling clouds, called sand storms.

Camel train

Saharan silver ants are shiny so their bodies can reflect the heat and keep them cool.

ABOVE AND BELOW

Although the Sahara looks empty, it's full of life. You just need to know where to look.

Desert monitor lizards like it hot – they come out of their burrows during the day to bask in the sun.

Zzzzzzz

Jerboas block the entrances to their burrows with sand to keep hot air – and other animals – out.

Fennec foxes sleep in burrows during the heat of the day.

...COOL NIGHTS

Lots of desert creatures come out at night to hunt.

Sharp-eyed owls snap up mice.

COME ON NOW, TIME FOR BED.

These people have built a tent using woven mats and wooden poles.

Thirsty animals stop to drink at an oasis – an area of desert where there is water and a few plants can grow.

Cape hares

Houbara bustard

A cheetah prowls the desert looking for its next meal.

Addax can take in all the water they need from eating plants and drinking morning dew.

Sand vipers move across the loose desert sands in winding, sideways motions.

ASIA

Reindeer

Wild Bactrian camels roam the bare, rocky canyons of the Gobi Desert.

Caspian Sea

DIZZYING HEIGHTS, pages 40-41
From snow-topped mountains to deep, icy valleys, the Himalayas form the world's highest mountain range.

Darjeeling

Arabian Sea

Red Sea

Kestrel

Mumbai

Bay of Bengal

HERE COMES THE RAIN, pages 42-43
All over India, farmers depend upon monsoon rains to water their crops.

Tamil Nadu

INDIAN OCEAN

Petra is an ancient city that was carved out of desert sandstone.

Stretching over 21,000km (13,000 miles), The Great Wall of China, is the longest structure ever built.

The tough larch trees of the Taiga – a huge, snowy forest – can survive long, frozen winters.

Sea of Japan

Yangtze River

Yellow River (Huang He)

Gobi horse

Giant panda

East China Sea

Philippine Sea

SHAKE, RATTLE AND ROLL, pages 44-45
Around 1,500 earthquakes strike Japan every year – from tiny shudders to enormous shakes that bring down whole buildings.

South China Sea

Built by ancient kings, the ruined temples of Angkor are the world's largest religious monument.

CREATURES OF THE DEEP, pages 46-47
All kinds of strange creatures lurk in the deepest, darkest waters of the Pacific Ocean.

Orangutan

Mount Semeru

DIZZYING HEIGHTS

Over a hundred snow-topped mountains rise high into the skies above South Asia. Together, they make up the Himalayas – the world's highest, and longest, mountain range.

In this shady hollow, a solid river of ice, called a glacier, slowly creeps downhill.

Glaciers form over tens of thousands of years, as layers of snow build up and squash down into thick ice.

Life up high can be tough – but around 70 million people live in the Himalayas.

Melted water from the glacier empties into a big lake.

HUP HUP

Farmers carve steps into the slope to grow rice. The steps stop soil from getting washed down the mountain.

Yak herders are always on the move. They keep yaks for their milk and meat, and use the wool to make clothes.

BRRRR!
It's freezing cold on the highest mountain tops...

...and the wind can blow up to

160km (100 miles) per hour.

AVALANCHE!

A massive pile of loose snow tumbles down the mountainside, crushing everything in its path.

Lush forests grow at the bottom of the mountains, where it's warm and sheltered from the wind.

ANIMALS OF THE HIMALAYAS

Only animals with very thick fur can survive on the snowy mountain tops...

...such as these Himalayan brown bears...

GRR

RARRR

...and this snow leopard.

Short, spiky grasses and shrubs carpet the rocky lower slopes.

BAAAAAA

Himalayan blue sheep scamper across the rocks, nibbling on grass.

A bearded vulture keeps its beady eyes out for little animals to snatch.

Marmots hide from hunters by scurrying into underground burrows where they sleep.

At the bottom of the mountains, red pandas snooze high up in the trees.

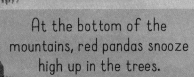

Markhor roam the forests, munching on grass and leaves.

HERE COMES THE RAIN

After months of hot, sticky weather, the skies darken over India and the wind starts to blow. It's the beginning of the summer monsoon – when heavy rain lashes across the country for around four months.

A monsoon is a seasonal change in wind direction. In India, a monsoon wind blows between June and September, bringing lots of rain.

MUMBAI

It's here! People welcome the start of the monsoon in the city of Mumbai. The rains bring relief from the blistering heat.

Sand bags are put out to stop water from flooding into the houses.

BUY YOUR UMBRELLAS HERE!

Auto rickshaw

HOORAY

Although people celebrate the monsoon, the streets can get badly flooded with water, and traffic grinds to a halt.

TAMIL NADU

Rice farmers in Tamil Nadu rely on the monsoon to flood their fields of rice. Rice needs lots of water to grow.

A rice field is called a paddy.

Strong oxen or water buffalo are used to dig trenches in the flooded fields, ready for planting.

DARJEELING

When the monsoon arrives in Darjeeling, tea pickers set to work, high in the lush green hills.

Tea is harvested by carefully plucking young tea shoots.

During the monsoon, a strong-tasting tea known as rain tea is ready to be plucked.

SHAKE, RATTLE AND ROLL

Earthquakes make the ground tremble and shake. Often they are hardly noticeable, but some are much more powerful – although these ones only happen in certain parts of the world. In Japan more than 1,500 earthquakes are recorded every year.

MOVING ROCK

Twelve enormous pieces of rock called plates sit on top of the Earth's crust (see page 25).

NORTH AMERICAN PLATE

PACIFIC PLATE

EURASIAN PLATE

Earthquakes happen when the moving plates slip or slide against each other.

Although you can't usually feel it, these plates are moving around, very, very slowly.

JAPAN

● Tokyo

Japan sits at the edge of four plates, which is why so many earthquakes happen here.

Earthquakes can be very dangerous.

PHILIPPINE PLATE

Wires, cables and pipes break up, so people don't have any power, light or heat.

Gas leaks can cause fires and broken water pipes can cause floods.

When the ground shakes, buildings, roads and bridges can collapse.

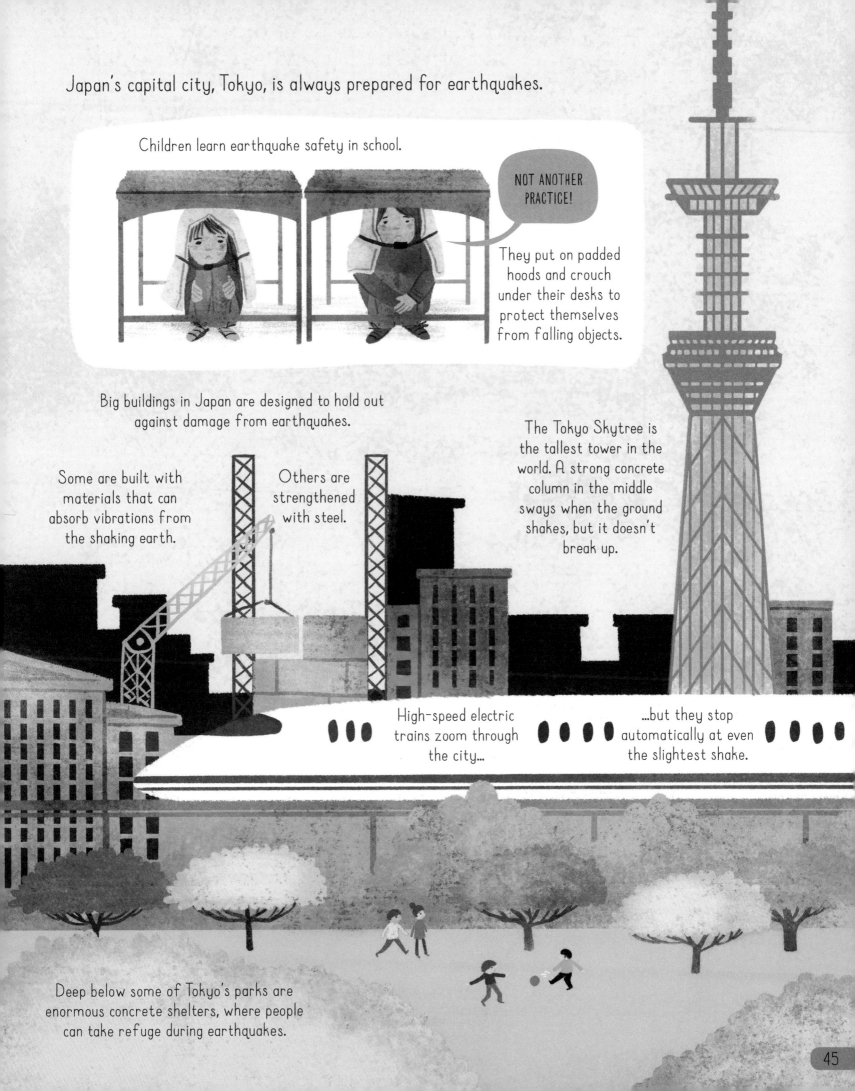

Japan's capital city, Tokyo, is always prepared for earthquakes.

Children learn earthquake safety in school.

NOT ANOTHER PRACTICE!

They put on padded hoods and crouch under their desks to protect themselves from falling objects.

Big buildings in Japan are designed to hold out against damage from earthquakes.

Some are built with materials that can absorb vibrations from the shaking earth.

Others are strengthened with steel.

The Tokyo Skytree is the tallest tower in the world. A strong concrete column in the middle sways when the ground shakes, but it doesn't break up.

High-speed electric trains zoom through the city...

...but they stop automatically at even the slightest shake.

Deep below some of Tokyo's parks are enormous concrete shelters, where people can take refuge during earthquakes.

CREATURES OF THE DEEP

Deep, deep down, far beneath the waves, the Pacific Ocean is very cold and very dark. All kinds of strange creatures live in these shadowy depths...

THE MIDNIGHT ZONE
1,000m (3,000ft) below the surface

Oceans are divided into layers, called zones. In the deepest zones, the dark water glitters and glows. Many of the animals that live here make their own light.

Lanternfish flash blue and green. They use their lights to find and attract mates.

HELLO, HELLO!

PING

PING

Stoplight loosejaw fish make a beam of red light that they use to explore the dark waters.

ARGH!

Shrimp can't see red light, so they are easily snapped up.

TZZ TZZ

Female anglerfish shine a light above their wide-open jaws to lure other fish inside...

A giant squid wiggles through the water, using its eight arms and two long tentacles to catch fish.

Giant squids truly are enormous. Their eyes alone are the size of dinner plates.

DUM DEE DUM...

Viperfish float along, waiting for hours until a tasty snack appears.

Giant tube worms attach themselves to the sea floor. They grow taller than a person.

Deep-sea pigs can fit into the palm of your hand. They aren't related to pigs – they're a type of animal called a sea cucumber.

This supergiant amphipod look like a shrimp – but it's 20 times bigger.

Hatchetfish

THE ABYSS

4,000m (13,000ft) below the surface

Even further down, it's pitch-black. Temperatures here are just above freezing.

Dumbo octopuses hover at the bottom of the ocean looking for worms and snails to eat. Their fins look like elephant ears.

Long-legged sea spiders scuttle along the ocean floor.

Snailfish are so pale, they're almost see-through.

TKK TKK TKK

DEEP-SEA TRENCH

6,000m (20,000ft) below the surface

Great holes in the ocean floor are called deep-sea trenches. The weight of the water here is crushing. Few people have been able to explore this deep...

...but some animals are still able to survive.

Big underwater chimneys, called black smokers, puff out very hot water.

Tree kangaroos climb from tree to tree in the lush jungles of New Guinea.

Mount Carstensz (Puncak Jaya)

Coral Sea

Timor Sea

ROOTS OF THE SEA, pages 50-51

Flooded forests of mangrove trees grow straight out of the sea along the coast of Australia.

INDIAN OCEAN

Uluru (Ayers Rock)

Koala

Red kangaroo

Murray River

Great Victoria Desert

FIRE, FIRE! pages 54-55

Every year, wildfires break out across the Australian bush, bringing destruction, but also new growth.

Great Australian Bight

Tasman Sea

Tasmanian devil

AUSTRALASIA

Goldband fusiliers

SHALLOW WATERS, pages 52-53
All kinds of tropical fish dart around the Great Barrier Reef – the largest group of corals in the world.

Bora Bora – also known as "the Pearl of the Pacific" – is a small island that rises from the shallow, sheltered waters of a glistening lagoon.

PACIFIC OCEAN

The dazzling city of Sydney is built around an enormous bay. Over five million people live here, making it Australia's biggest city.

Humphead wrasse

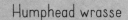

Volcanoes rise up in the middle of the Tongariro National Park, which is also scattered with hot springs and steam vents.

Mount Cook

Kiwi

ROOTS OF THE SEA

Along the warm coasts of Northern Australia, spidery trees called mangroves grow in swamps created by ocean tides that wash through every day. All kinds of creatures scramble and swim through these muddy forests.

PEEP PEEP

Lesser noddy birds build plush nests from mangrove leaves.

Mangrove roots sink into the gloopy mud. They stop the trees from being pulled over by ocean waves.

Mangrove monitor lizard

MMM

Mangrove jack

Saltwater crocodiles cruise through the water where there are lots of tasty creatures to snap up...

Baby fish shelter between tangled roots to keep away from hungry animals.

Banded sea kraits weave through the knotted roots.

These fruits are called mangrove apples.

Black flying foxes are actually a type of big bat. During the day they hang fast asleep from mangrove branches, safe from hungry hunters down below.

ZZZZZZZZ

False water-rats live at the bottom of mangrove trees where they build nests out of mud and leaves.

Mangrove orchids

The roots that stick out of the water are called breathing roots. They take in oxygen from the air.

SQUELCH SQUELCH

Mudskippers are a type of fish that can live both in and out of water. They crawl across the mud on their fins – and can even climb trees.

Black tiger shrimp

Barramundi

Mud lobsters hide in burrows in the mud during the day.

SHALLOW WATERS

In warm, shimmering waters off the coast of Eastern Australia, the sea floor is covered with billions of tiny creatures, called corals. Together, they make up the Great Barrier Reef – the biggest group of corals in the world.

A green sea turtle warms itself near the surface of the sunny waters.

Lots of sea creatures live in and around the Great Barrier Reef.

Corals grow in groups, making strange shapes that look like plants.

This little pufferfish has a secret trick...

...it can puff itself into a big spiky ball to scare off hunters.

Spotted eagle ray

Angelfish

Some corals are soft and bendy, while others are hard and stony.

This humphead wrasse holds a spiky sea urchin in its mouth, to crack it open against a rock.

TAP TAP

Lionfish

Hermit crab

Sea anemones are animals with stinging tentacles.

Clownfish hide between sea anemone tentacles. The stings don't hurt them.

CORAL, CORAL EVERYWHERE

Over 400 types of coral
live in the Great Barrier Reef.
Here are some of them:

Staghorn coral

Branched finger coral

Mushroom coral

Toadstool coral

Honeycomb coral

Yellow scroll coral

Blue coral

Cabbage coral

Tube coral

Sea fan

Brain coral

Pearl bubble coral

Flowerpot coral

Elegance coral

Sea pen

FIRE, FIRE!

Every year in Australia, wildfires sweep through vast areas of grassland, scrub and forest known as the bush, burning almost everything in their path. Although they're very dangerous, these fires help to keep the bush healthy by encouraging new plants to grow.

A small number of wildfires are triggered by lightning strikes.

Trees and grasses grow quickly during wet weather.

As the weather becomes hotter and drier, plants dry out and wildfires can start easily.

Dry grass, leaves and twigs burn quickly, allowing the wildfires to spread.

Most wildfires are started accidentally – by people dropping lit cigarettes or using machines that give off sparks.

Kangaroos escape from fires as soon as they smell smoke.

Eucalyptus trees have oily leaves that burn easily. These trees rely on heat from the fire to release their seeds.

POP!

The eucalyptus seed pods explode in the heat, scattering seeds across the ground.

Black kites are also known as firehawks because they dive into fires to hunt insects and lizards fleeing the heat.

Wildfires leave huge clouds of ash hanging in the air, which sometimes turn the sky red.

STEADY... STEADY...

Small wildfires burn themselves out, but bigger ones can rage out of control and cause lots of damage. Firefighters drop water from helicopters to try to put them out.

The soil that's left behind after the fire is rich with ash, which helps plants grow.

Wombats burrow under the ground to escape the flames.

Thick leaves around the bases of Australian grass trees keep their roots safe from fires. Some grass trees even flower after being burned.

After a fire, cycad plants have lots of sunlight, space and rich soil to grow in.

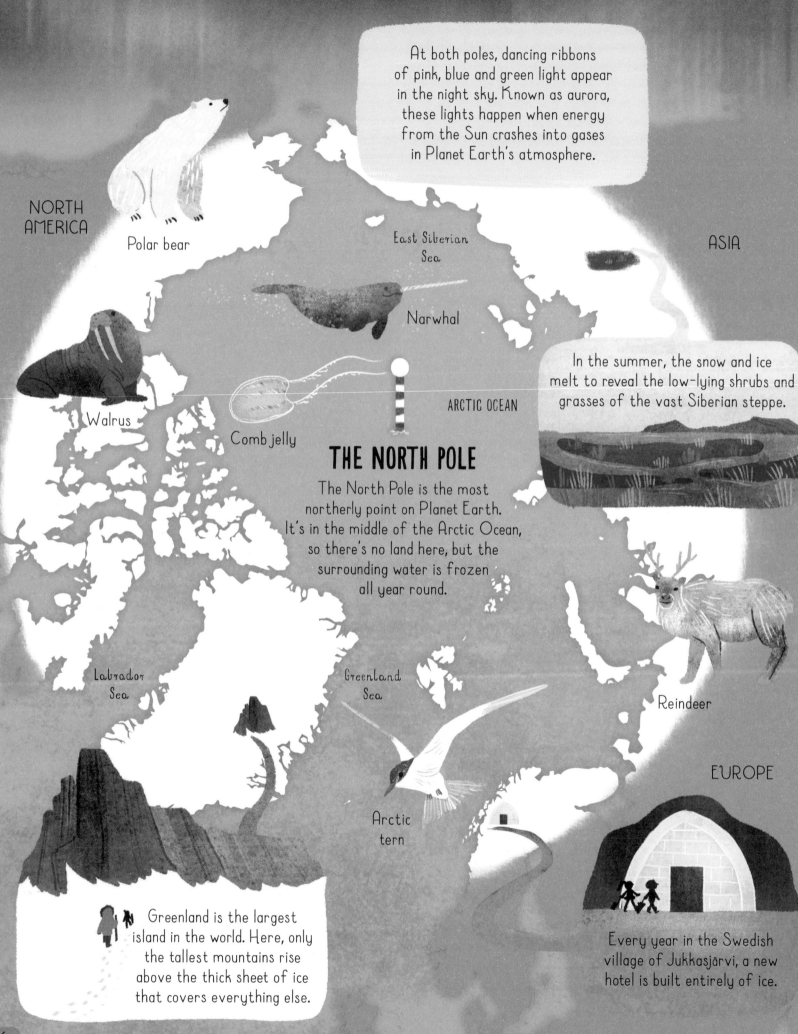

At both poles, dancing ribbons of pink, blue and green light appear in the night sky. Known as aurora, these lights happen when energy from the Sun crashes into gases in Planet Earth's atmosphere.

NORTH AMERICA

Polar bear

East Siberian Sea

ASIA

Narwhal

In the summer, the snow and ice melt to reveal the low-lying shrubs and grasses of the vast Siberian steppe.

Walrus

Comb jelly

ARCTIC OCEAN

THE NORTH POLE

The North Pole is the most northerly point on Planet Earth. It's in the middle of the Arctic Ocean, so there's no land here, but the surrounding water is frozen all year round.

Reindeer

Labrador Sea

Greenland Sea

EUROPE

Arctic tern

Greenland is the largest island in the world. Here, only the tallest mountains rise above the thick sheet of ice that covers everything else.

Every year in the Swedish village of Jukkasjärvi, a new hotel is built entirely of ice.

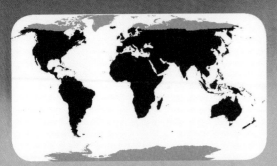

THE NORTH & SOUTH POLES

THE BIG FREEZE, pages 58-59
Nearly all life on this frozen continent is found along its coasts, where gigantic sheets of ice stretch out over the ocean.

ANTARCTICA

Mount Erebus is the southernmost volcano in the world that still erupts.

Albatross

THE SOUTH POLE
The most southerly point on Planet Earth is the South Pole – it's in the middle of a huge continent called Antarctica.

Transantarctic Mountains

Weddell Sea

Ross Sea

Weddell seal

Ellsworth Mountains

Emperor penguins

Turquet's octopus

Hourglass dolphin

SOUTHERN OCEAN

The Antarctic Peninsula is the warmest part of the continent. For a few weeks in summer, it's the only place where plants can grow.

THE BIG FREEZE

Antarctica is a whole continent that is almost entirely covered by ice. It is the coldest, driest and emptiest place on Planet Earth and much of it has never been explored...

Antarctica doesn't belong to any single country and no one lives there all the time.

It never rains on Antarctica and it very rarely snows. This ice has built up over hundreds of thousands of years.

All the animals in Antarctica live in, or near, the sea. Only a few birds fly far inland.

In some places, the ice is nearly 5km (3 miles) thick. The oldest, deepest ice is more than a million years old.

The ice doesn't just stop when the land ends. It reaches far out over the sea, like an enormous shelf.

Scientists from all over the world come to visit for a while to study the land, its weather and its wildlife.

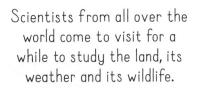

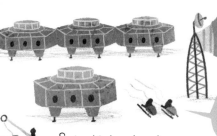

Scientists stay in research stations like this one.

RACE YOU TO THE BOAT!

Every winter, the whole ocean around Antarctica freezes over and the continent more than doubles in size.

At its biggest, the frozen ocean covers an area that's larger than South America.

Sometimes, chunks of ice break off and float away on the water. These chunks are called icebergs.

PENGUIN PARADE

These are four types of penguins that live in Antarctica:

Gentoo penguins make over 400 dives every day to find food in freezing ocean waters.

Chinstrap penguins move about on land by sliding across the ice on their bellies.

Adélie penguins make nests from stones. Parents take turns to look after their eggs.

Emperor penguins often huddle together for hours at a time to keep warm.

LOOKING AFTER PLANET EARTH

Planet Earth has everything we need to survive. There's fresh air to breathe, food to eat and water to drink. It is up to everyone who lives on our planet to look after what we have.

TAKING FROM PLANET EARTH

People use soil from the land to grow crops to eat.

Wood from trees is used to build and make things, from buildings and furniture to the paper in this book.

Metals and stones from the ground are used for building and making things.

Seas and oceans provide people with food, electricity and even medicines.

Water for drinking and growing crops falls as rain that flows into rivers, lakes and underground springs.

People need energy to make electricity and provide power to make machines work.

Most energy comes from burning fuels such as coal, oil or gas.

Burning fuels pollutes the planet by making the air dirty...

...BUT there are cleaner ways to make energy.

Light from the Sun – solar power

Wind power

Rushing water – hydro power

Heat from under the ground – geothermal energy (see page 25)

WHAT CAN YOU DO FOR PLANET EARTH?

The future of our amazing planet – and everything that lives on it – depends on us.
We must act now before it's too late.

Think twice before buying plastic bottles and other things made of plastic.

Our oceans are full of plastic that has been thrown away.

This plastic is killing huge numbers of animals who can get caught up in it, or poisoned, if they mistake it for food.

If we don't change the way we use plastic, the future of all life on Planet Earth will be at risk.

Try to recycle things instead of throwing them away. Recycling is when old objects are used to make something new.

Many things can be recycled, including plastic, paper, glass and metal.

You can also reduce the amount of energy and other materials you take from the Earth.

Switch off lights and other machines when they're not in use.

Don't waste water.

Buy things without much packaging so there's less waste.

Try not to take so many car journeys.

Try to find ways to reuse what you already have.

Use leftover packaging for arts and crafts.

Take your own bags with you when you go shopping.

Save fruit and vegetable peelings to make food – called compost – for growing plants.

Give away old toys or clothes for someone else to use.

Small changes can make a BIG difference. By doing what we can and working together, we can save Planet Earth.

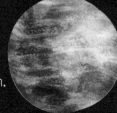

INDEX

Editor: Ruth Brocklehurst

Managing Designer: Stephen Moncrieff **Digital designer:** John Russell

Expert consultants: Dr. Roger Trend, Dr. Zoe Simmons, Jenny Slater

First published in 2019 by Usborne Publishing Ltd., Usborne House, 83-85 Saffron Hill, London, EC1N 8RT, United Kingdom. www.usborne.com Copyright © 2019 Usborne Publishing Ltd.
The name Usborne and the devices ⚲ 🎈 are Trade Marks of Usborne Publishing Ltd. All rights reserved.
No part of this publication may be reproduced, stored in any retrieval system, or transmitted in any form or by any means, electronic, mechanical, photocopying, recording or otherwise, without the prior permission of the publisher. UKE.